THE PEACEMAKER

Exploring the Enneagram 9

Asa Eccleston Kibilski

CONTENTS

THE HEART OF PEACE: WELCOMING THE ENNEAGRAM 9

Have you ever felt like the glue that holds everything together, the silent observer in a room full of voices, or the one who prioritizes harmony above all else? Perhaps you've noticed a tendency to merge with others, adapting to their preferences and avoiding conflict at all costs. If these resonate with you, then you might just be an Enneagram 9, also known as the Peacemaker.

The Enneagram, an ancient system of personality typing, offers a profound map for self-discovery and understanding. At its core, the Enneagram isn't about labeling or boxing people in; it's about illuminating the underlying motivations, fears, and desires that shape our unique ways of being in the world. And the Enneagram 9, with their gentle spirit and innate ability to foster peace, holds a special place within this intricate tapestry.

The Peacemaker's Heart's Desire: At the heart of every Enneagram 9 lies a deep longing for inner peace and harmony. They yearn for a sense of oneness with themselves, others, and the world around them. This desire for connection often manifests in their remarkable capacity for empathy, compassion, and acceptance. Nines have an uncanny ability to see the good in everyone and everything, creating a sense of safety and belonging wherever they go.

The Peacemaker's Core Fear: Beneath their peaceful exterior, Nines carry a fear of separation and conflict. They worry about being overlooked, neglected, or losing their sense of inner peace. This fear can lead them to avoid confrontation, suppress their own needs, and go along with the flow, even when it goes against their own values or desires.

The Body Center: Grounding the Peacemaker: The Enneagram

is not just about personality; it's also deeply connected to our instincts and bodily sensations. Nines belong to the Body Center, which means they are attuned to their physical needs and the comfort of their environment. This grounding influence helps them stay connected to the present moment and find solace in simple pleasures.

The Wings of the Dove: The 8 and 1 Influence: Nines are not a monolithic group; they come in different flavors, shaped by the neighboring types on the Enneagram circle. The 8 wing brings a touch of assertiveness and a willingness to take charge, while the 1 wing infuses a sense of idealism and a desire for order and integrity. Understanding your wing can provide valuable insights into your unique strengths and challenges.

Embarking on a Journey of Self-Discovery: As we delve deeper into the world of the Enneagram 9, we will explore their core motivations, fears, and desires in greater detail. We will examine the ways in which they navigate relationships, work, and personal growth. We will uncover the challenges they face and offer practical tools for self-care and well-being. Most importantly, we will celebrate the Peacemaker's unique gifts and encourage them to embrace their power to create harmony and healing in the world.

So, if you're ready to embark on a journey of self-discovery and embrace your inner Peacemaker, let's dive in together. This is your invitation to explore the depths of your being, understand your unique wiring, and cultivate a life filled with authenticity, peace, and joy.

THE BODY CENTER: GROUNDING THE PEACEMAKER

Imagine yourself as a majestic oak tree, roots deeply embedded in the earth, swaying gently in the breeze, providing shade and shelter to all who seek refuge beneath its branches. This image beautifully captures the essence of the Enneagram 9's connection to the Body Center, also known as the Instinctive Center.

The Body Center is one of the three centers of intelligence in the Enneagram, alongside the Head Center (thinking) and the Heart Center (feeling). It governs our basic survival instincts, physical needs, and our relationship with the material world. For Nines, this center is their primary source of energy and grounding.

The Grounded Presence of the Nine: Nines are known for their calm and steady demeanor, often emanating a sense of tranquility that soothes those around them. This grounded presence stems from their strong connection to the Body Center. They are attuned to their physical sensations, aware of their need for rest and nourishment, and drawn to activities that engage their senses and connect them to the present moment.

The Simple Pleasures of Life: Nines find joy in the simple pleasures of life, such as spending time in nature, enjoying delicious food, or engaging in creative activities that involve touch and movement. They appreciate the beauty of everyday routines and rituals, finding comfort and stability in the familiar. This appreciation for the tangible world helps them stay grounded and centered, even when faced with challenges or uncertainty.

The Body as a Source of Wisdom: For Nines, the body is not just a vessel for carrying out tasks; it's a source of wisdom and guidance. They often have a deep intuitive understanding of their physical needs and can sense when something is out of balance.

This somatic intelligence can be a valuable tool for self-care and well-being, helping them make choices that support their overall health and happiness.

The Challenge of Numbness: While their connection to the Body Center is a source of strength, it can also be a potential challenge for Nines. When faced with conflict or overwhelming emotions, they may unconsciously disconnect from their bodies as a way to protect themselves. This can manifest as numbness, apathy, or a tendency to "go with the flow" even when it doesn't align with their true desires.

Cultivating Body Awareness: To navigate this challenge, Nines can benefit from cultivating greater body awareness. This can involve practices such as mindfulness meditation, yoga, or any activity that helps them tune into their physical sensations and emotions. By consciously reconnecting with their bodies, Nines can access their inner wisdom, make more authentic choices, and tap into their full potential.

The Body as a Bridge to Peace: Ultimately, the Body Center serves as a bridge to the inner peace that Nines so deeply crave. By honoring their physical needs, engaging their senses, and listening to the wisdom of their bodies, Nines can cultivate a sense of grounded presence and well-being that radiates outward, touching the lives of everyone they encounter.

As we continue our exploration of the Enneagram 9, we will delve deeper into the unique ways in which their Body Center influences their relationships, work, and personal growth. We will offer practical tools and practices for cultivating greater body awareness and using this connection to create a life filled with peace, joy, and fulfillment.

WINGS OF THE DOVE: THE 8 AND 1 INFLUENCE

Imagine a dove, gracefully soaring through the sky, its wings outstretched, each feather contributing to its effortless flight. This image beautifully illustrates the concept of wings in the Enneagram, where the neighboring types on either side of a core type subtly influence its expression. For the Enneagram 9, the Peacemaker, these wings are the assertive and energetic 8, the Challenger, and the principled and idealistic 1, the Reformer.

The 8 Wing: The Assertive Peacemaker Nines with an 8 wing often exhibit a quiet strength and a surprising capacity for action. While they may still prioritize harmony, they are not afraid to speak their minds or take a stand when necessary. The 8 wing infuses them with a dose of assertiveness, empowering them to set boundaries, advocate for themselves, and even take on leadership roles.

These Nines may have a natural ability to mediate conflicts, using their calm demeanor and understanding of both sides to find common ground. They are often drawn to careers that involve helping others, such as counseling, social work, or teaching. In personal relationships, they tend to be supportive and loyal, offering a safe space for loved ones to express themselves.

However, the 8 wing can also present challenges. Nines with this wing may struggle with anger and resentment, especially when their needs are repeatedly overlooked. They may find it difficult to say no, leading to overcommitment and burnout. By embracing their assertive side and learning to express their emotions in healthy ways, they can find a balance between their desire for peace and their need for self-expression.

The 1 Wing: The Idealistic Peacemaker Nines with a 1 wing are often guided by a strong sense of integrity and a desire for fairness and justice. They have high standards for themselves and others, striving for excellence in all areas of life. The 1 wing infuses them with a sense of purpose and direction, motivating them to make a positive impact on the world.

These Nines may be drawn to careers that align with their values, such as environmental activism, social justice advocacy, or the arts. In personal relationships, they tend to be supportive and encouraging, inspiring others to reach their full potential.

However, the 1 wing can also create challenges. Nines with this wing may struggle with perfectionism and self-criticism, feeling like they are never good enough. They may become overly focused on rules and regulations, losing sight of the bigger picture and the needs of those around them. By learning to embrace their imperfections and cultivate a more compassionate inner voice, they can find a balance between their desire for order and their need for acceptance.

Embracing Both Wings While the 8 and 1 wings offer distinct strengths and challenges, it's important to remember that all Nines possess both wings to some degree. The key is to recognize and integrate both aspects of your personality. By embracing your assertive side, you can advocate for yourself and create healthy boundaries. By embracing your idealistic side, you can find purpose and meaning in your life.

By cultivating a deeper understanding of your wings, you can unlock a greater sense of self-awareness and personal growth. You can learn to navigate the complexities of your personality with grace and authenticity, using your unique gifts to create a life filled with peace, purpose, and joy. Remember, you are not just a Peacemaker; you are a Peacemaker with the power to inspire and transform the world around you.

THE ART OF MERGING: THE 9'S PATH TO CONNECTION

Imagine a river gently flowing into a vast ocean, its waters blending seamlessly, becoming one with the greater whole. This image encapsulates the essence of merging, a core aspect of the Enneagram 9's way of being in the world.

At the heart of merging lies a deep-seated desire for connection and belonging. Nines long to feel at one with others, to create a sense of harmony and unity in their relationships. This desire can manifest in various ways, from subtle acts of accommodation to a profound sense of oneness with loved ones.

Merging as a Survival Strategy: For many Nines, merging is a learned behavior that originated in childhood as a way to maintain peace and avoid conflict. Perhaps they grew up in a family where their needs were overshadowed by the needs of others, or where disagreements were quickly swept under the rug. As a result, they learned to adapt to the preferences of others, suppressing their own desires and opinions in order to keep the peace.

Merging in Relationships: In intimate relationships, Nines often prioritize the needs and desires of their partners, sometimes at the expense of their own. They may go along with their partner's plans, even if it means sacrificing their own preferences. This can create a sense of closeness and intimacy, but it can also lead to resentment and a loss of individuality if the Nine's needs are consistently neglected.

Merging in the Workplace: In the workplace, Nines are known for their collaborative spirit and ability to get along with everyone. They are natural team players, willing to compromise and find solutions that benefit the group as a whole. This can make them valuable assets to any organization, but it can also lead to them being overlooked or undervalued if they don't assert themselves.

The Shadow Side of Merging: While merging can be a powerful tool for connection, it can also become a trap if taken to extremes. When Nines habitually prioritize the needs of others over their own, they risk losing touch with their own desires, opinions, and sense of self. This can lead to feelings of emptiness, frustration, and even resentment.

Finding a Healthy Balance: The key to healthy merging lies in finding a balance between connection and autonomy. Nines need to learn to honor their own needs and desires, while still remaining open and receptive to the needs of others. This requires developing a strong sense of self, setting clear boundaries, and learning to say no when necessary.

Embracing Individuality: While the desire for connection is a fundamental part of the Nine's nature, it's important to remember that they are also unique individuals with their own thoughts, feelings, and perspectives. By embracing their individuality and expressing themselves authentically, Nines can deepen their relationships, enhance their creativity, and live a more fulfilling life.

The Journey of Self-Discovery: The journey towards healthy merging is a process of self-discovery and growth. It involves exploring the roots of your merging tendencies, identifying the situations where you are most likely to lose yourself, and developing strategies for staying grounded and connected to your own truth.

Remember, merging is not a weakness; it's a superpower. By learning to wield this power with awareness and intention, Nines can create harmonious relationships, build strong communities, and ultimately, fulfill their deepest desire for connection and belonging.

FINDING YOUR VOICE: OVERCOMING THE NUMBNESS

Imagine a beautiful melody trapped within a silent instrument, yearning to be heard, yet unable to break free. This image poignantly captures the struggle many Enneagram 9s face when it comes to expressing their own needs, desires, and opinions.

The Tendency Towards Numbness: Nines are often described as peacemakers, harmonizers, and mediators. Their natural inclination is to create a sense of calm and avoid conflict at all costs. However, this desire for peace can sometimes lead to a form of emotional numbness, where they suppress their own feelings and needs in order to maintain harmony in their relationships and environment.

The Origins of Numbness: This tendency towards numbness often stems from childhood experiences, where Nines may have learned to prioritize the needs of others over their own. Perhaps they grew up in a family where expressing emotions was discouraged, or where conflict was quickly swept under the rug. As a result, they developed a habit of suppressing their own feelings and going along with the flow, even when it didn't align with their true desires.

The Impact on Relationships: While this strategy may have served them well in the past, it can create challenges in their adult relationships. When Nines consistently prioritize the needs of others over their own, they risk losing touch with their own desires and opinions. This can lead to feelings of resentment, frustration, and even anger, which can further complicate their relationships.

The Importance of Finding Your Voice: Finding your voice is a crucial step in the Enneagram 9's journey of self-discovery and personal growth. It involves recognizing and expressing your own needs, desires, and opinions, even when it feels uncomfortable or inconvenient. It means learning to say no when necessary and setting healthy boundaries in your relationships.

Overcoming the Fear of Conflict: One of the biggest obstacles to finding your voice is the fear of conflict. Nines often worry that expressing their own needs will upset others or disrupt the peace. However, healthy conflict is a natural part of any relationship. By learning to express their feelings in a constructive way, Nines can actually strengthen their relationships and create a deeper sense of intimacy and connection.

Tips for Finding Your Voice:

- **Start small:** Begin by expressing your opinions or preferences in low-stakes situations, such as choosing a restaurant or movie to watch.
- **Practice assertiveness:** Learn to say no when you don't want to do something, and don't be afraid to ask for what you need.
- **Use "I" statements:** When expressing your feelings, focus on your own experience rather than blaming or accusing others. For example, instead of saying "You always ignore my needs," try saying "I feel unheard when my needs are not considered."
- **Seek support:** Talk to a trusted friend, therapist, or Enneagram coach who can help you explore your feelings and develop healthy communication skills.
- **Be patient:** Finding your voice takes time and practice. Don't get discouraged if you don't see results immediately. Keep practicing, and eventually, you will find your own unique way of expressing yourself.

Remember, your voice is a powerful tool for creating positive change in your life and in the world. By embracing your own needs, desires, and opinions, you can live a more authentic and fulfilling life, and inspire others to do the same.

INNER HARMONY: CULTIVATING PRESENCE AND PEACE

Imagine a calm lake reflecting the vast expanse of the sky, its surface undisturbed by ripples or waves. This image embodies the inner harmony that Enneagram 9s, the Peacemakers, seek to cultivate within themselves and their surroundings.

The Nine's Innate Serenity: Nines possess a natural inclination towards tranquility and balance. They are often drawn to peaceful environments, soothing activities, and harmonious relationships. Their presence can be calming and grounding for those around them, as they exude an aura of serenity that seems to quell anxieties and dissolve tensions.

The Challenge of Inner Turmoil: However, beneath this calm exterior, Nines may experience a quiet inner turmoil. Their desire for harmony can lead them to suppress their own emotions and needs, creating a disconnect between their inner and outer worlds. This can manifest as feelings of emptiness, numbness, or a sense of being lost or unmoored.

Cultivating Inner Peace: To overcome this challenge, Nines need to cultivate a deeper sense of inner peace and connection to their authentic selves. This involves developing practices that help them tune into their emotions, identify their needs, and express themselves authentically.

Mindfulness and Meditation: One of the most powerful tools for cultivating inner peace is mindfulness meditation. This practice involves paying attention to the present moment without judgment, observing thoughts and feelings as they arise and pass away. Regular mindfulness practice can help Nines become more aware of their inner landscape, identify triggers for emotional numbness, and cultivate a deeper sense of self-awareness.

Connecting with the Body: Another important aspect of cultivating inner peace is connecting with the body. Nines are often so focused on maintaining external harmony that they neglect their own physical and emotional needs. Engaging in activities that promote body awareness, such as yoga, tai chi, or dance, can help them reconnect with their bodies and tap into their inner wisdom.

Spending Time in Nature: Nature has a unique ability to soothe the soul and restore inner balance. Nines can benefit from spending time in natural settings, whether it's walking in the woods, sitting by a river, or simply gazing at the stars. The sights, sounds, and smells of nature can help them slow down, de-stress, and connect with a sense of peace that transcends the busyness of everyday life.

Creative Expression: Engaging in creative activities, such as painting, writing, music, or crafts, can also be a powerful way for Nines to express themselves and connect with their inner world. Creativity allows them to tap into their emotions and explore their unique perspectives in a safe and non-threatening way.

Cultivating Gratitude: Practicing gratitude can also enhance inner peace. By focusing on the positive aspects of their lives and acknowledging the good in others, Nines can cultivate a sense of contentment and well-being. This can be as simple as keeping a gratitude journal, sharing appreciation with loved ones, or taking time each day to reflect on the things they are grateful for.

The Ripple Effect of Inner Peace: As Nines cultivate greater inner peace and harmony, they not only benefit themselves, but also those around them. Their calm and centered presence can have a ripple effect, creating a more peaceful and harmonious environment for everyone they interact with.

By embracing their innate serenity and cultivating practices that nourish their inner peace, Nines can truly embody their role as Peacemakers, bringing harmony and healing to the world around them.

NAVIGATING CONFLICT: THE 9'S GUIDE TO PEACEMAKING

Imagine a dove perched between two sparring hawks, its presence a calming balm amidst the tension. This image embodies the innate peacemaking abilities of Enneagram 9s, who often find themselves drawn to mediate conflicts and restore harmony in their relationships and communities.

Conflict Avoidance vs. Conflict Resolution: While Nines are naturally averse to conflict, it's important to distinguish between conflict avoidance and conflict resolution. Avoidance involves ignoring or suppressing disagreements, often leading to resentment and unresolved issues. Resolution, on the other hand, involves acknowledging and addressing the underlying causes of conflict, with the goal of finding mutually agreeable solutions.

The Nine's Peacemaking Superpowers: Nines possess a unique set of skills that make them natural peacemakers. Their empathy and compassion allow them to understand different perspectives, their patience and diplomacy help them navigate difficult conversations, and their calm demeanor can de-escalate tense situations.

The Art of Mediation: When conflict arises, Nines can act as mediators, creating a safe space for all parties to express their feelings and needs. They can help clarify misunderstandings, identify common ground, and facilitate compromise. Their ability to see the bigger picture and focus on shared goals can be invaluable in resolving disputes and restoring harmony.

The Importance of Self-Care: While Nines are skilled at mediating conflicts between others, they often struggle to address their own needs and concerns. It's important for them to remember that self-care is not selfish, but essential for their own well-being and their ability to effectively help others. Nines need to create space for their own emotions and needs, set healthy boundaries, and avoid overextending themselves.

Finding Your Voice: In order to be effective peacemakers, Nines need to find their own voice. This means learning to express their own opinions and needs assertively, even when it feels uncomfortable or risks upsetting others. It also means setting clear boundaries and learning to say no when necessary.

Embracing Healthy Conflict: While Nines naturally gravitate towards peace and harmony, it's important for them to recognize that conflict is a natural part of life. In fact, healthy conflict can be a catalyst for growth and change. By learning to embrace conflict as an opportunity for deeper understanding and connection, Nines can transform their relationships and communities.

Tips for Navigating Conflict as a Nine:

- **Acknowledge your feelings:** Don't suppress your emotions, even if they are uncomfortable. Allow yourself to feel anger, sadness, or frustration, and express those feelings in a healthy way.
- **Set clear boundaries:** Let others know what you are and are not willing to tolerate. Don't be afraid to say no when necessary.
- **Practice active listening:** When someone is expressing their feelings, listen attentively and try to understand their perspective.
- **Avoid taking things personally:** Remember that conflict is not a personal attack. Try to see the situation from the other person's point of view.
- **Focus on solutions:** Instead of dwelling on the problem, brainstorm possible solutions that meet everyone's needs.
- **Seek compromise:** Be willing to give a little to get a little. Remember, the goal is to find a solution that works for everyone.
- **Celebrate successes:** When you successfully navigate

a conflict, take a moment to acknowledge your efforts and celebrate your progress.

By embracing their peacemaking abilities and learning to navigate conflict with grace and compassion, Nines can create a more harmonious world, one relationship at a time.

RELATIONSHIPS: NURTURING HARMONY AND AVOIDING INDIFFERENCE

Imagine a tapestry woven with threads of different colors and textures, each strand contributing to the overall beauty and strength of the fabric. This image reflects the intricate and interconnected nature of relationships in the life of an Enneagram 9, the Peacemaker.

The Nine's Relational Superpowers: Nines are natural nurturers, often described as the "glue" that holds relationships together. Their empathy, compassion, and ability to see all sides of a situation make them excellent listeners and supportive partners. They have a gift for creating a sense of warmth, acceptance, and belonging, making others feel valued and appreciated.

Nines also possess a remarkable ability to adapt to the needs of others, often prioritizing their partners' preferences over their own. This can create a sense of harmony and ease in relationships, but it can also lead to challenges if the Nine's own needs are consistently neglected.

The Challenge of Indifference: One of the biggest challenges Nines face in relationships is the risk of slipping into indifference. When their own needs are consistently suppressed, they may become emotionally distant and disengaged. This can lead to a lack of passion and excitement in their relationships, leaving both partners feeling unfulfilled.

Balancing Harmony and Individuality: To create thriving relationships, Nines need to find a balance between their desire for harmony and their need for individuality. This involves learning to express their own needs and desires, setting healthy boundaries, and communicating their feelings honestly and openly.

Nines can also benefit from cultivating a deeper sense of self-awareness and recognizing when they are sacrificing their own needs for the sake of peace. By prioritizing self-care and engaging in activities that nourish their souls, they can bring more vitality and passion to their relationships.

Navigating Different Relationship Dynamics: Nines may find themselves drawn to partners who are more assertive and decisive, as they complement their own laid-back nature. However, it's important for Nines to choose partners who respect their boundaries and appreciate their need for harmony.

In friendships, Nines are often valued for their loyalty, supportiveness, and ability to create a sense of community. They enjoy spending time with friends, engaging in shared activities, and creating lasting memories. However, it's important for Nines to ensure that their friendships are reciprocal and that they are not always the ones giving more than they receive.

Family Dynamics: Within families, Nines often play the role of peacemaker, mediating conflicts and maintaining harmony. They may have a special bond with their siblings, acting as confidants and supporters. However, it's important for Nines to establish healthy boundaries with family members and avoid taking on too much responsibility for their emotional well-being.

Cultivating Healthy Communication: One of the keys to healthy relationships for Nines is cultivating open and honest communication. This involves expressing their feelings, needs, and desires in a clear and direct way, while also being receptive to feedback from their partners. By creating a safe space for dialogue and vulnerability, Nines can deepen their connections and build stronger, more fulfilling relationships.

Embracing the Power of Love: Nines are often described as having a heart of gold. Their capacity for love, compassion, and acceptance is a gift to the world. By embracing their unique relational superpowers and learning to balance harmony with individuality, Nines can create a ripple effect of love and healing in their relationships and communities.

Remember, relationships are a two-way street. By prioritizing your own needs and expressing yourself authentically, you can create a space for your partner to do the same. This mutual respect and understanding can lead to deeper intimacy, greater connection, and a shared sense of joy and fulfillment.

WORK AND PURPOSE: FINDING FULFILLMENT WITHOUT LOSING YOURSELF

Imagine a potter gently shaping clay on a wheel, their hands intuitively guiding the form, their mind focused on the present moment. This image captures the essence of the Enneagram 9's approach to work and purpose, where the focus is on finding fulfillment and meaning without sacrificing their core values and sense of self.

The Nine's Strengths in the Workplace: Nines bring a unique set of strengths to the workplace. Their natural ability to create harmony and foster collaboration makes them valuable team players. They are patient listeners, empathetic problem-solvers, and skilled mediators. Their calm demeanor and aversion to conflict can help defuse tense situations and create a more positive work environment.

Nines are also often drawn to careers that involve helping others, such as counseling, teaching, healthcare, or social work. Their compassionate nature and desire to make a difference in the world can be a driving force in their professional lives.

The Challenge of Merging with the Job: However, the Nine's tendency to merge with others can pose a challenge in the workplace. They may find themselves adapting to the expectations and preferences of their colleagues and superiors, even if it means compromising their own values or goals. This can lead to a loss of identity and a sense of being adrift in their careers.

Finding a Purposeful Path: To avoid merging with their jobs and find true fulfillment, Nines need to connect with their deeper purpose and values. This involves identifying their passions, interests, and skills, and seeking out work that aligns with their unique gifts and talents.

Nines may find it helpful to explore different career paths and experiment with various roles and responsibilities. They can also benefit from seeking guidance from mentors or career coaches who can help them identify their strengths and weaknesses and develop a clear career vision.

Balancing Work and Life: Another important aspect of finding fulfillment in work is maintaining a healthy work-life balance. Nines often have a tendency to overextend themselves, taking on more responsibilities than they can handle. This can lead to burnout and a loss of passion for their work.

To avoid this, Nines need to set clear boundaries between their work and personal lives. This might involve setting limits on work hours, delegating tasks, and prioritizing time for rest, relaxation, and self-care. By maintaining a healthy balance, Nines can ensure that they are able to bring their best selves to their work, while also enjoying a fulfilling personal life.

Embracing Your Unique Gifts: Ultimately, finding fulfillment in work is about embracing your unique gifts and using them to make a positive impact on the world. Nines have a special ability to create harmony, foster collaboration, and inspire others. By sharing their talents and passions, they can create a more peaceful and fulfilling work environment for themselves and their colleagues.

Remember, your work is not just a job; it's an opportunity to express your creativity, connect with others, and make a meaningful contribution to society. By following your heart, honoring your values, and maintaining a healthy work-life balance, you can create a career that is both personally rewarding and professionally successful.

GROWTH PATH: AWAKENING TO YOUR TRUE POTENTIAL

Imagine a caterpillar nestled within its chrysalis, undergoing a profound transformation, unseen by the outside world. This metamorphosis mirrors the journey of growth and self-discovery that awaits the Enneagram 9, the Peacemaker, as they awaken to their true potential.

The Nine's Path of Integration: In the Enneagram, each type has a direction of growth, a path towards greater wholeness and integration. For the Nine, this path leads towards the healthy traits of the Enneagram 3, the Achiever. This doesn't mean that Nines become Threes; rather, they integrate the healthy aspects of the Three into their own personality.

Embracing Healthy Ambition and Action: Healthy Threes are known for their drive, ambition, and ability to take action. They are goal-oriented, focused, and motivated to achieve success. By integrating these qualities, Nines can overcome their tendency towards inertia and procrastination, and move towards their goals with greater confidence and determination.

Developing a Stronger Sense of Self: Healthy Threes also possess a strong sense of self and a clear understanding of their values and priorities. They are able to assert themselves, set boundaries, and make decisions that align with their goals. By developing these qualities, Nines can overcome their fear of conflict and express their needs and desires more confidently.

Finding Focus and Direction: One of the challenges Nines face on their growth path is finding focus and direction. They may struggle with prioritizing their goals, getting sidetracked by distractions, or feeling overwhelmed by the sheer number of possibilities. By learning to set clear priorities, break down large goals into smaller steps, and focus on one task at a time, Nines can overcome these challenges and move towards their goals with greater ease and efficiency.

Overcoming the Fear of Success: Another challenge for Nines is the fear of success. While they may have a deep desire to achieve their goals, they may also worry about the potential consequences of success, such as increased responsibility, visibility, or conflict. By addressing these fears and recognizing their own worth and capabilities, Nines can embrace their full potential and step into their power.

Celebrating Achievements and Learning from Mistakes: Healthy Threes are not afraid to celebrate their achievements and acknowledge their hard work. They also recognize that mistakes are a natural part of the learning process and use them as opportunities for growth. By adopting this mindset, Nines can overcome their tendency towards self-deprecation and learn to appreciate their own accomplishments.

Cultivating Resilience and Perseverance: The path of growth is not always easy, and there will be setbacks and challenges along the way. By cultivating resilience and perseverance, Nines can overcome these obstacles and continue moving towards their goals. They can draw strength from their inner peace and connection to their values, and find support from loved ones and mentors.

The Journey of a Lifetime: The journey of growth is a lifelong process, and there is no one-size-fits-all approach. However, by embracing the healthy aspects of the Enneagram 3, Nines can tap into their hidden potential, overcome their challenges, and create a life that is both fulfilling and meaningful. Remember, growth is not about becoming someone you're not; it's about becoming the best version of yourself.

STRESS AND HEALTH: THE 9'S VULNERABILITY AND RESILIENCE

Imagine a serene pond, its surface reflecting the surrounding beauty, yet beneath the calm lies a hidden ecosystem with its own vulnerabilities and resilience. This image mirrors the Enneagram 9's relationship with stress and health, where a peaceful exterior often masks underlying stressors and unique coping mechanisms.

The Stress Response of the Nine: Nines are known for their aversion to conflict and their desire for inner peace. However, this doesn't mean they are immune to stress. In fact, their tendency to suppress their own needs and emotions can create a build-up of internal tension that can manifest in physical and emotional symptoms.

Under stress, Nines may become increasingly withdrawn and passive, prioritizing the needs of others over their own to maintain harmony. This can lead to a sense of emotional numbness, apathy, and a lack of motivation. They may also experience physical symptoms such as fatigue, headaches, digestive problems, and sleep disturbances.

The Link Between Stress and Health: Research has shown a strong link between chronic stress and a variety of health problems, including heart disease, high blood pressure, obesity, and depression. Nines, with their tendency to internalize stress, may be particularly vulnerable to these conditions.

Furthermore, Nines may also struggle with addictive behaviors as a way to cope with stress. They may turn to food, alcohol, drugs, or other substances to numb their emotions and create a sense of temporary peace.

Cultivating Resilience: Despite their vulnerabilities, Nines also possess remarkable resilience. Their innate optimism, adaptability, and ability to find joy in simple pleasures can help them weather the storms of life. By cultivating healthy coping mechanisms and addressing the root causes of their stress, Nines can build resilience and protect their physical and emotional well-being.

Strategies for Stress Reduction: Nines can benefit from a variety of stress reduction techniques, such as mindfulness meditation, yoga, deep breathing exercises, and spending time in nature. Regular exercise can also help reduce stress and improve overall health.

Therapy and Support Groups: For Nines who struggle with chronic stress or addiction, therapy and support groups can provide valuable guidance and support. Therapists can help Nines identify the root causes of their stress, develop healthy coping mechanisms, and cultivate a stronger sense of self. Support groups can provide a safe space for Nines to share their experiences and connect with others who understand their struggles.

Mindful Eating and Movement: Nines are often drawn to the comforts of food and may use eating as a way to soothe themselves or avoid dealing with difficult emotions. However, emotional eating can lead to weight gain and other health problems. By practicing mindful eating, Nines can learn to tune into their bodies' hunger and fullness cues and make healthier food choices.

Regular physical activity can also be a powerful stress reliever for Nines. Engaging in activities they enjoy, such as walking, dancing, or swimming, can help them release pent-up emotions, boost their mood, and improve their overall well-being.

The Importance of Self-Compassion: One of the most important aspects of stress management for Nines is cultivating self-compassion. They need to learn to be kind to themselves, forgive their mistakes, and recognize their own worth and value. By treating themselves with the same love and compassion they extend to others, Nines can create a foundation for healing and resilience.

Remember, taking care of your health is not a luxury; it's a necessity. By prioritizing self-care, addressing stress in healthy ways, and cultivating a positive mindset, Nines can live a life of joy, vitality, and well-being.

THE SPIRITUAL 9: CONNECTING TO INNER PEACE AND WISDOM

Imagine a vast, starlit sky, its twinkling lights revealing a glimpse of the infinite mystery and wonder of the universe. This image reflects the spiritual depth and intuitive nature of the Enneagram 9, the Peacemaker, who often possesses a profound connection to something greater than themselves.

The Nine's Innate Spirituality: Nines are often described as having an "old soul" quality. They possess a quiet wisdom, a deep appreciation for the interconnectedness of all things, and a yearning for spiritual connection. This innate spirituality may manifest in a variety of ways, from a love of nature and meditation to a fascination with mystical traditions and philosophies.

The Nine's Intuitive Gifts: Nines are also often gifted with intuition, a subtle knowing that transcends logic and reason. They may have a knack for sensing the underlying emotions and motivations of others, or a sense of knowing what is right or true in a given situation. This intuitive guidance can be a valuable asset in their personal and professional lives, helping them make wise decisions and navigate complex situations.

Spiritual Practices for Nines: There are many spiritual practices that can help Nines deepen their connection to their inner wisdom and cultivate a sense of peace and well-being. These practices may include:

- **Meditation:** Meditation can help Nines quiet their minds, connect with their inner stillness, and access deeper levels of awareness.
- **Mindfulness:** Practicing mindfulness, or paying attention to the present moment without judgment, can help Nines

become more aware of their thoughts, feelings, and bodily sensations.

- **Yoga and Tai Chi:** These gentle forms of exercise can help Nines connect with their bodies, release tension, and cultivate a sense of groundedness.
- **Spending Time in Nature:** Nature has a calming and restorative effect on many Nines, helping them feel more connected to the natural world and the divine presence within it.
- **Creative Expression:** Engaging in creative activities, such as painting, writing, music, or dance, can be a powerful way for Nines to express their spirituality and connect with their inner world.
- **Spiritual Reading and Study:** Exploring spiritual texts and teachings can provide Nines with inspiration, guidance, and a deeper understanding of their own spiritual path.
- **Service to Others:** Helping others is a core value for many Nines. Engaging in acts of service, whether it's volunteering at a local shelter or simply offering a listening ear to a friend in need, can be a deeply fulfilling spiritual practice.

The Nine's Spiritual Challenges: While Nines are naturally drawn to spirituality, they may also face certain challenges on their spiritual path. Their desire for peace and harmony can sometimes lead them to avoid facing difficult emotions or confronting challenging situations. This can hinder their spiritual growth and prevent them from fully embracing their potential.

Another challenge for Nines is the tendency to merge with the beliefs and practices of others. While it's important to be open to different perspectives, Nines need to discern which spiritual practices resonate with them personally and avoid simply going along with the crowd.

Finding Your Own Path: The most important thing for Nines on their spiritual journey is to find their own unique path. This may involve exploring different spiritual traditions, experimenting with various practices, and seeking guidance from trusted mentors or teachers.

The ultimate goal is to cultivate a deep and meaningful connection to the divine presence within themselves and in the world around them. By embracing their spirituality, Nines can tap into their inner wisdom, discover their true purpose, and create a life that is both meaningful and fulfilling.

INTEGRATING THE SHADOW: EMBRACING ANGER AND DESIRE

Imagine a calm lake reflecting a cloudless sky, its surface unruffled. Yet, beneath the tranquility, dark currents stir, hidden depths that hold emotions and desires that can seem at odds with the peaceful exterior. This imagery mirrors the inner landscape of the Enneagram 9, the Peacemaker, who, in their pursuit of harmony, may unconsciously suppress darker aspects of their personality – their anger and desire.

The Peacemaker's Shadow: The shadow, in the context of the Enneagram, refers to those aspects of ourselves that we often deny, repress, or project onto others. For the Peacemaker, this shadow often encompasses anger and desire. These emotions can seem threatening to the Nine's core desire for peace and harmony, and as a result, they may be pushed down into the unconscious.

The Suppression of Anger: Nines are often known for their easygoing nature and aversion to conflict. However, beneath this calm exterior, anger can simmer. When their needs are consistently ignored or boundaries are repeatedly crossed, anger can build up, even if it's not consciously acknowledged. This suppressed anger can manifest in passive-aggressive behaviors, resentment, or even physical ailments.

The Fear of Desire: Nines may also suppress their desires, fearing that expressing them will disrupt the peace or create conflict. They may believe that their wants and needs are not important, or that they don't deserve to have them met. This can lead to a sense of emptiness, a lack of motivation, and a feeling of being disconnected from their own authentic selves.

The Importance of Integrating the Shadow: Integrating the shadow is a crucial step in the Nine's journey of self-discovery and personal growth. By acknowledging and accepting their anger and desire, Nines can reclaim these lost parts of themselves and tap into their full potential.

Embracing Anger: Anger, when expressed healthily, can be a powerful force for change and self-assertion. Nines can learn to express their anger in ways that are respectful and constructive, using it to set boundaries, advocate for themselves, and fight for what they believe in. This can lead to a greater sense of empowerment and a deeper connection to their own inner strength.

Honoring Desire: By honoring their desires, Nines can tap into their passion and motivation, and create a life that is more fulfilling and meaningful. This involves recognizing their own needs and wants, giving themselves permission to pursue their dreams, and learning to say "yes" to the things that bring them joy.

Tips for Integrating the Shadow:

- **Self-Reflection:** Take time to reflect on your emotions and identify when you are feeling angry or suppressing your desires.
- **Journaling:** Write about your feelings in a journal to help you process and understand them.
- **Therapy or Coaching:** Seek guidance from a therapist or coach who can help you explore your shadow and develop healthy ways of expressing your emotions.
- **Creative Expression:** Use creative outlets, such as painting, writing, or music, to express your anger and desires in a safe and constructive way.
- **Mindfulness:** Practice mindfulness to become more aware of your emotions as they arise and to observe them without judgment.

Remember, your shadow is not something to be feared, but rather a part of yourself that needs to be acknowledged and integrated. By embracing your anger and desire, you can unlock a greater sense of wholeness, authenticity, and personal power.

THRIVING AS A 9: PRACTICAL TOOLS FOR DAILY LIFE

Imagine a toolbox filled with a variety of instruments, each designed for a specific purpose, each essential for building and maintaining a sturdy, well-functioning structure. This image reflects the practical tools and strategies that Enneagram 9s, the Peacemakers, can utilize to thrive in their daily lives, fostering inner peace, enhancing relationships, and achieving their goals.

1. **Prioritize Self-Care:** As natural caretakers, Nines often put the needs of others before their own. However, prioritizing self-care is not selfish; it's essential for maintaining physical, emotional, and spiritual well-being. Make time for activities that nourish your soul, whether it's reading a good book, taking a relaxing bath, spending time in nature, or simply enjoying a quiet moment of reflection.

2. **Set Clear Boundaries:** One of the biggest challenges for Nines is learning to say "no." Setting clear boundaries is crucial for protecting your energy and preventing burnout. It's okay to decline requests that don't align with your priorities or values. Remember, saying "no" to something you don't want to do is saying "yes" to yourself.

3. **Practice Mindful Decision-Making:** Nines can sometimes struggle with making decisions, fearing that they might upset others or disrupt the peace. Practicing mindful decision-making involves tuning into your intuition, considering your values and priorities, and weighing the potential consequences of each choice.

Remember, it's okay to take your time and trust your gut instinct.

4. **Cultivate Healthy Communication:** Open and honest communication is essential for building strong relationships and maintaining inner peace. Practice expressing your feelings, needs, and opinions in a clear and assertive way. Avoid passive-aggressive behavior, and learn to address conflicts directly and respectfully.

5. **Create Routines and Rituals:** Routines and rituals can provide a sense of structure and stability, which can be especially grounding for Nines. Create daily or weekly routines that incorporate self-care, exercise, creative expression, and time for relaxation and connection with loved ones.

6. **Find a Creative Outlet:** Engaging in creative activities, such as painting, writing, music, or dance, can be a powerful way for Nines to express themselves, release emotions, and connect with their inner world. Make time for creativity in your daily life, and explore different forms of expression to find what resonates with you.

7. **Connect with Nature:** Spending time in nature can be incredibly restorative for Nines. The peace and tranquility of the natural world can help calm the mind, soothe the soul, and reconnect with a sense of inner peace. Make a habit of taking walks in the park, hiking in the woods, or simply sitting in your backyard and appreciating the beauty around you.

8. **Cultivate Gratitude:** Practicing gratitude can have a profound impact on your overall well-being. Take time each day to reflect on the things you are grateful for,

whether it's your health, your loved ones, your home, or the simple pleasures of life. Gratitude can help shift your focus from what you lack to what you have, cultivating a sense of contentment and joy.

9. **Embrace Mindfulness:** Mindfulness involves paying attention to the present moment without judgment. It can be practiced in many ways, such as meditation, yoga, or simply taking a few deep breaths and noticing the sensations in your body. Mindfulness can help you become more aware of your thoughts and emotions, cultivate self-compassion, and connect with a sense of inner peace.

10. **Seek Support:** Don't be afraid to ask for help when you need it. Talk to a trusted friend, therapist, or Enneagram coach who can provide support, guidance, and encouragement. Remember, you don't have to go through life alone. There are people who care about you and want to see you thrive.

By implementing these practical tools into your daily life, you can create a more peaceful, fulfilling, and joyful existence. Remember, thriving as a Nine is not about perfection; it's about embracing your unique gifts, honoring your needs, and cultivating a life that aligns with your values and aspirations.

EMBRACING YOUR PEACEMAKER POWER: A FINAL REFLECTION

Imagine a world where peace isn't merely a dream, but a lived reality. A world where understanding and compassion triumph over conflict and division. This is the world that Enneagram 9s, the Peacemakers, envision and strive to create. As we reach the end of our journey exploring the depths of the Peacemaker's heart, let us take a moment to reflect on the profound gifts and potential that reside within each and every Nine.

A Beacon of Hope and Healing: Nines are not simply peace-lovers; they are peace-makers, actively working to cultivate harmony in their relationships, communities, and the world at large. Their gentle nature, their capacity for empathy, and their unwavering belief in the inherent goodness of humanity make them a beacon of hope in a world that often feels fractured and divided.

Nines have a unique ability to see the bigger picture, to find common ground between seemingly opposing viewpoints, and to create a space where everyone feels heard and valued. Their presence is like a balm, soothing the wounds of conflict and fostering an atmosphere of trust and understanding.

Embracing Your Gifts: As a Nine, you have a powerful gift to offer the world. Your ability to create harmony, mediate conflict, and foster connection is essential for building a more peaceful and compassionate society. Embrace your unique strengths and use them to make a positive impact on the world around you.

Remember that your voice matters, even if it's quiet. Your gentle nature is not a weakness, but a source of strength. Your ability to see the good in everyone is a precious gift, and your unwavering belief in the possibility of peace is a powerful catalyst for change.

Challenges and Opportunities: While Nines possess incredible gifts, they also face unique challenges on their path to growth and fulfillment. The tendency to merge with others, suppress their own needs, and avoid conflict can hinder their personal development and lead to feelings of emptiness and dissatisfaction.

However, these challenges also present opportunities for growth. By embracing their shadow, learning to set boundaries, and finding their own voice, Nines can step into their full power and create a life that is both peaceful and fulfilling.

The Journey Continues: The journey of self-discovery is never truly over. As you continue to explore your Enneagram type, you will undoubtedly uncover new layers of understanding and insight. Embrace this ongoing journey with curiosity, compassion, and a willingness to learn and grow.

Remember, you are not alone on this path. There are countless other Nines who are also striving to live a more authentic and fulfilling life. Seek out community and support from those who understand your unique strengths and challenges.

A Final Word of Encouragement: As we close this chapter, I want to leave you with a final word of encouragement. Embrace your Peacemaker power. Trust in your intuition. Believe in your ability to make a difference. And remember, you are a precious and valuable part of this world.

May you continue to shine your light brightly, spreading peace, love, and understanding wherever you go. The world needs your gifts now more than ever.